Sunflowers Always Face the Light

P. Nicole Gilbert

BookLeaf Publishing

India | USA | UK

Presentation by *BookLeaf Publishing*

Web: www.bookleafpub.com

E-mail: info@bookleafpub.com

ISBN: 9789357214094

First edition 2022

For mom, thanks for believing in me.

ACKNOWLEDGEMENT

I would like to give a special thanks to my mom who gave me the encouragement I needed to take this massive step as a writer. I also want to thank my dad and brother who, along with my mom, have supported my passion for writing. Lastly, I want to thank my grandma. She has been my partner in crime for my entire life, as well as a caregiver and best friend. She has always pushed me to be my very best and I could never ask for a better person by my side.

i knew

the stars were bright in the sky that night
not a sound for miles
besides our slow breaths
the wind blew softly
rustling our hair
i didn't have to meet your eyes
to know you were looking at me
our hands intertwined
with no intent on letting go
the man in the moon
the only witness to this moment
the moment i knew i never wanted to be
in anyone else's arms but yours

when men give us moments

the feeling of being desired for a second
is nothing compared to days of feeling worthless
being in his embrace behind closed doors
cannot overshadow the secrecy he shows the
outside world
the light from your fleeting smile
does not overcome the dark nights of
tear-stained cheeks
the constant confusion of being lost
does not fade away with one line of vague
directions
kisses from his lips on your skin
do not heal the bruises on your body and mind
minimal words of affirmation
crumble in the presence of his loveless actions
we must not choose to stay
when our despair is blanketed by the temporary,
inconsistent
moments of reprieve he gives

annihilation

barren ground fills vast expanses of our once
green earth
with miles upon miles of devastation to the flora
and fauna
rocks and dirt inhale all the water like a sponge
leaving nothing for the wildlife to thrive
animals venture on a mission
in search of a viable source of food
but cannot survive to complete the journey
starvation plagues the world like a disease
virtually destroying everything it touches
droughts stretch over countries and continents
and icebergs cry silent tears as heat levels rise
stabbing mother earth in her once flourishing
heart
jungles of skyscrapers have replaced forests of
trees
while factories pollute our oxygen with deadly
toxins
oceans have become human's favorite junkyard
and thousands of species are rapidly declining
humanity was supposed to be the world's savior
instead, we have become its annihilation

skin

i still remember how it felt to touch your skin
melting into mine at every crease and bend
as if the heavens made us for just one another
i still remember the coarse feeling of your face
so gloriously imperfect
yet undeniably perfect for me
i still remember every place
your skin touched mine
forever marked like a permanent tattoo

wasn't you

i was with him today
but he wasn't you
he stole my breath away with his kiss
but he wasn't you
he held my hand
but he wasn't you
he hugged me tightly
but he wasn't you
he made me laugh
but he wasn't you
he told me he loved me
but he wasn't you
i tried to love him back
but he wasn't you

6/24/22

there is no adequate way
to describe the feeling of despair
when the world crashes at our feet
and humanity's balance begins to crumble
when the powerful wolves
attack the rabbit
even though she has already lost the fight
and the lines between friend and foe
blur into a mist of utter destruction
when the knights that swore to protect us
slash their weapons down our backs
a tidal wave plummets the princesses of the
kingdom
and the knights use their powerful swords
to stake not only the bellies of the princesses
but their very souls

during that time

during that time
we felt utter loneliness
the only real friend our devoted shadow
the days were endless
and the nights too long
with the entire world at a standstill
we lost our ability to naturally socialize
the only form of communication
was through a pixelized screen
school was a job that had lost all its meaning
and finding the strength to get up
was our toughest task
we kept our distance
when we needed a human's touch the most
and struggled to find the light
at the end of the opaque tunnel
we are forever tainted with the lives of the
artificial
and society will be altered until the end
no matter how much time will pass

eyes

your eyes used to be so easy to get lost in
a beautiful clear blue like a shimmering summer
lake
that i was eager to swim to the depths of
in the past, your hands fit so perfectly in mine
the calluses that signified your hard work and
character
they seemed so rough compared to my soft ones
yet there was nothing quite so perfectly matched
back then your laugh was so contagious
it played in my mind like a symphony on
constant repeat
even after i closed my eyes at night
your smile was so genuine
that i couldn't look away
for fear that it wouldn't be seared into my mind
forever
how is it that after all this time
it's hard to imagine those features that consumed
my every thought
and the man who let his personality shine
through them
how is it that after all the hours i used to spend
staring into your eyes

i can no longer remember their exact shade of
blue

a simple answer

you made me feel accepted
and appreciated
and pretty
you told me i was funny
and that i am nice
you wanted me to meet your family
and you sometimes smiled at me
you hugged me for many minutes
and made me grin
you really liked me
you asked me why i don't want to start again
the answer was quite simple
he makes me feel adored
and treasured
and gorgeous
he tells me that i am hilarious
and that i am selfless
he embraces me as his family
and he always smiles with me
he hugs me for hours
and makes me shine
he really loves me

inhale, exhale

heart beating a mile a minute
palms becoming moist
with the perspiration of fear
head pounding ferociously
sending panic alarms to my brain
body stiff, shocked and unmovable
tears running like a waterfall
mouth dry, unable to beg for assistance
the overwhelming feeling of helplessness
will entirely consume me
it feels as if the stress will never dissipate
i'm okay
calm down
think positively
inhale
exhale
breathe

beauty

a flower is effortless in her beauty
every intricate detail unique to her
her colors are radiant
with petals of the most vibrant of hues
and stems and leaves to accentuate her figure
even though she is lovely on the outside
it pales in comparison to her dazzling qualities
inside
she is strong and determined
and she is selfless and considerate
a flower is confident and sophisticated
and dances so alluringly to the music of the wind
she is incredibly welcoming and caring
and is stunning inside even more than out
why is it that even though she has so much to
offer
she only gets picked because of her outer
beauty?

stranger

how can a familiar face become so
unrecognizable?
how can a once infectious laugh become so
distant?
how can a calming disposition become so
unsettling?
how can secrets become so easily unlocked?
how can a safe space become so dangerous?
how can a once loving embrace become so
malicious?
how can a person's approachable eyes become so
withdrawn?
how can a human's touch become treachery?
how can a conflict become the doom of a
friendship?
how can a sister become a complete stranger?

fear of betrayal

i hated that i craved another's love
but couldn't accept it for fear of betrayal
the butterflies swarmed in my stomach at first
in anticipation of newness and joy
now the butterflies have decayed
and left uneasiness and uncertainty in its wake
no matter how often you tell me i'm pretty
i feel that i would never be startling enough
i am quick witted and humorous
but i fear that i am not as interesting as other
girls
the more i fall for a person
the more i'm terrified of the climb back up
and punish my own self by becoming withdrawn
i allow my insecurities to consume me like a
tsunami
even though i'm aware that i am self-imploding
and my partner is hit with the remaining
shrapnel
i just can't control it
i don't know if i ever will

prettiest black dress

i wore my prettiest black dress for you
even though you wouldn't go with me
i did my hair and makeup
i made sure to wear my best necklace
and strutted around in my expensive shoes
i smiled the whole night
even though you weren't there
the anticipation for you was overwhelming
because i knew i'd see you once it was over
and everyone was gone
i couldn't wait for your eyes to land on me
but when they did
your mouth stayed shut
i really hate that dress

us women

us women are elegant
and strong
and capable
us women are fierce
and loyal
and kind
us women are intelligent
and nurturing
and hilarious
us women are brave
and loving
and sexy
us women are warriors
and saints
and indestructible

home

i always believed that i would find
the most comfort in a building
or a specific location
or in a materialistic thing such as an object
however, i've never felt the most at peace
until i saw your eyes
and felt your embrace
and heard your laugh
i've never felt so strong
until i felt your kiss
and watched your dazzling smile
and listen to you speak
home is not a physical place
it's with you

pride

it is incomprehensible why humanity puts
so much emphasis
on a small thing called pride
friendships
wealth
love
all put on the line for something so simple
yet incredibly complicated
pride speaks for us
when we need our voice the most
and takes the words out of our mouths
to dissolve in the air, unsaid
pride is a labyrinth of complexities in the mind
that fuel our natural instinct
to discover what we believe makes us fulfilled
but instead, is the roadblock of what we really
need
by overshadowing and condemning
our true happiness

someday...

someday someone will embrace me
without holding a knife to my back
someday someone will accept my family
instead of pretending they were ghosts
someday someone will shine the light
on my dark, anxious mind
someday someone will see me in their future
instead of as a temporary past time
someday someone will smile at me with pride
and not turn away when i am imperfect
someday someone will let me fly
and fix my broken wings
someday someone will truly love me for me
because i deserve nothing less